THE ART OF MAKING SENSE
Writings and Speeches 2019

By
Andrew Klavan

ISBN: 9781705836644

Table of Contents

Can We Believe?..5

Can We Be Silent In A World
    Gone Mad?...19

The Art of Making Sense..32

Speaking Across the Abyss: Building Culture in an Age of
    Unbelief...43

Can We Believe?

A version of this article appeared in City Journal, *Spring 2019 Issue*

The West is falling. Quietly, politically, without a violent upheaval, the Islamists are taking control of France. A dissolute literature professor named Francois retires to a monastery near Poitiers, the place where Charles Martel stopped the last advance of Islam in 732. A man at once mesmerized and dejected by the sensual pleasures of cultural decadence, Francois is seeking to reconnect with the Christian religion that formed the great French culture of the past.

But faith in that religion will not come to him. "I no longer knew the meaning of my presence in this place," he says of the monastery. "For a moment, it would appear to me, weakly, then just as soon it would disappear."

He leaves the monastery, ready to convert to Islam and submit to the new order.

"I'd be given another chance; and it would be the chance at a second life, with very little connection to the old one," he says. "I would have nothing to mourn."

*

This sequence from Michel Houellebecq's controversial 2015 novel *Submission* is a near perfect fictional representation of a phenomenon I've noticed in many intellectuals since the latest rise of militant Islam. These thinkers see the great days of the West ending while a mean, violent, intolerant religion infests its ruins. They believe Europe has lost the will to live, and that loss is linked to a loss of faith in Christianity. But while they yearn to see the West revived — and while they may even support Christianity as a social good or a metaphorical vehicle for truth — they cannot themselves believe.

*

Why We Should Call Ourselves Christians, a 2008 essay by Italian philosopher and politician Marcello Pera, is the clearest example of this phenomenon. Written in response to 9/11, it depicts a Europe paralyzed by self-hating lassitude, willing to pay homage to any culture but its own.

"The West today is undergoing a profound moral and spiritual crisis, due to a loss of faith in its own worth, exacerbated by the apostasy of Christianity now rife within Western culture," Pera writes.

He goes on: "Without faith in the equality, dignity, liberty, and responsibility of all men — that is to say, without a religion of man as the son and image of God ... — liberalism cannot defend the fundamental and universal rights of human beings or hope that human beings can coexist in a liberal society. Basic human rights must be seen as a gift of God ... and hence pre-political and non-negotiable ..."

This sounds like the *cri de coeur* of a passionate believer, the sort of thing we used to hear from Europhile Pope Benedict XVI, who contributed the essay's introduction. But not so. The essay's title gives the game away. Pera could have called it *Why We Should Be Christians.* But he is an atheist. He accepts philosopher Emmanuel Kant's famous argument that God is necessary to the existence of morality. But from this he reasons, not that we must have faith, but that "we must live ... as if God existed."

Urgently needed as Christianity may be, he cannot believe.

In 2017's *The Strange Death of Europe,* Douglas Murray finds the death spiral of Muslim aggression and Western self-hatred still more advanced. Witness, just for one example, the Muslim rape gangs in Rotherham and elsewhere that abused thousands of local girls while authorities turned a blind eye for fear of being called racist.

Like Pera, Murray understands that the loss of Christian faith is a powerful contributor to "the problem in Europe of an existential tiredness and a feeling that perhaps for Europe the story has run out and a new story must be allowed to begin."

"Unless the non-religious are able to work with, rather than against, the source from which their culture came, it is hard to see any way through," Murray writes. "After all, though people may try, it is unlikely that anyone is going to be able to invent an entirely new set of beliefs."

But Murray too is a non-believer, as he told me explicitly during a conversation on my podcast. Again, he knows faith is needed, but he cannot believe.

Psychologist Jordan Peterson has become a popular phenomenon by riding the horns of this dilemma. His videos, his speeches, and his bestselling self-help book *12 Rules for Life: An Antidote to Chaos* all argue for imbuing life with the meaning and morality Kant maintained must be logically attached to the existence of God. But when it comes to declaring his actual beliefs, he is evasive.

"I act as if God exists," he says in one video, echoing Pera. "Now, you can decide for yourself whether that means that I believe in Him."

If I must decide for myself, I think Peterson is a Jungian. Beneath his abstruse verbiage, the Swiss psychiatrist Carl Jung essentially re-imagined spirituality as an emanation of the deepest truths of human experience. ("We cannot tell," he wrote, "whether God and the unconscious are two different entities.") In practice, this means the Jungian god is ultimately a metaphor, a means of externalizing our collective unconscious and its "archetype of wholeness." No amount of evasive verbalization can disguise the weakness of a metaphorical god. He is the signifier of human meaning as opposed to a living objective Presence who is the source of that meaning.

So even while attempting to address the Western crisis of will brought on by our loss of faith, Peterson too, I suspect, cannot truly believe.

*

What stands between these minds and their maker? Peterson, for one, rebels against the question "*Do you believe in God?*" because he says, "It's an attempt to box me in ... The question is asked so that I can be firmly placed on one side of a binary argument."

But this strikes me as unsound. All statements of belief box a thinker in. If the world is round, it cannot also be flat. And if there is objective morality and meaning in that world, it must have an ultimate objective source. To live "as if there were a God" is essentially to insist on the conclusions of a syllogism the premises of which you reject. Pera and Peterson notwithstanding, this makes no sense, and arguments that make no sense eventually collapse.

Murray's objection to faith, however, is more coherent. He believes that science and historical criticism have done "most likely irreversible damage ... to the literal-truth claims of religion." If he is right, it makes no difference whether or not faith is required, faith is impossible. You can't ask a society to pretend to believe in what isn't actually so.

But is Murray right? Have science and criticism truly undermined Christianity? Or is it simply that disbelief has become the intellectual's default conviction? To me, it seems highly possible that faith is being thwarted by a powerful social narrative that insists Christianity can't thrive in the modern world as we know it.

This narrative — let's call it the Enlightenment Narrative — has been with us now for centuries. It goes something like this:

The fall of Rome in the fifth century AD plunged the West from Classical civilization into cultural darkness. For the next thousand years, the Church encouraged superstition, stifled intellectual freedom, and repressed scientific inquiry. With the Renaissance of Classical learning, reason was set free, science was discovered, and faith was left behind as we marched into a world of wonders.

This Enlightenment Narrative had its beginnings as a sort of humanist propaganda campaign. Terms like *Dark Ages* and *Middle Ages* were created at the very start of the Renaissance (a loaded term in itself). They were meant to solidify the new generation's self-congratulatory idea that they had relit the fire of knowledge after a dark "middle" period.

The campaign worked. The Enlightenment Narrative has dominated the Western mind for half a millennium. It is the context in which Don Quixote went mad trying to imitate old chivalric values out of keeping with the new reality. It is why Shakespeare imagined a Hamlet stranded without certainty in the sudden absence of clear moral truth. It is why Hegel declared that "trust in the eternal laws ... has vanished," and Nietzsche proclaimed that "God is dead." And while many mighty minds — like Coleridge, Dostoevsky, C.S. Lewis and Pope Benedict XVI — have protested that no, even in the enlightened world, God still lives, the prevailing sense among thinking elites has been the one expressed by Matthew Arnold's *Dover Beach:* the Sea of Faith, once at full tide, is inexorably receding with a "melancholy, long, withdrawing roar."

The latest proclaimers of this narrative reject even the melancholy. The vision of these new minds stands in direct opposition to the morbid predictions of observers like Houellebecq, Pera, and Murray.

For them, the West and the world are doing great — better than ever — and the death of Christianity is a big part of the reason.

Steven Pinker's *Enlightenment Now* makes this case with gusto. These are the best of times, he says. We live, quite suddenly, in a world of "newborns who will live more than eight decades, markets overflowing with food, clean water that appears with a flick of a finger and waste that disappears with another, pills that erase a painful infection, sons who are not sent off to war, daughters who can walk the streets in safety, critics of the powerful who are not jailed or shot, the world's knowledge and culture available in a shirt pocket."

Reason and science — which "led most of the Enlightenment thinkers to repudiate a belief in an anthropomorphic God who took an interest in human affairs" — are not the cause of our dissolution but the founders of our feast.

Indeed, Pinker believes reports of the death of Western civilization are greatly exaggerated. He dismisses such pessimism as a fashionable intellectual pose fueled by negative biases in human cognition. "The world has made spectacular progress in every single measure of human well-being," he argues, and he says that progress is likely to continue as long as we live out the Enlightenment Narrative and leave religion behind.

*

But while Pinker's optimism is appealing, it is not entirely convincing. I have questions about his assessment of the present. Is increasingly atheistic Europe — especially Scandinavia — really the "gold standard" of happiness, pacifism and human rights, as he maintains? Or is it rather a moribund client culture wholly dependent on the military might, scientific inventiveness, and financial strength of the far more religious United States? Without the Bible-thumping U.S., wouldn't enlightened Europe quickly find itself overrun by Russian or

Chinese oppressors? Perhaps the pessimists are right, and it is being overrun right now by a slow-motion Islamic invasion which could end with our enlightened optimists silenced mid-hurrah.

As for the future: All throughout the triumphant strains of *Enlightenment Now*, I kept thinking of Rudyard Kipling's poem *Recessional*, written for Queen Victoria's Diamond Jubilee. At that moment in 1897, England specifically and Europe in general, were, like the West today, celebrating cultural and scientific achievements unmatched in all the history of humankind to that point. And yet Kipling, no devout a believer himself, marked the occasion by warning his countrymen against atheistic pride, praying:

> Lord God of Hosts, be with us yet,
> Lest we forget — lest we forget!

Lest we forget that not all intellectual misgivings are as baseless as Pinker says, just seventeen years after the poem was penned, Europe was engulfed in the three-decade cataclysm of world war that brought its cultural dominance to an end — war exacerbated by the anti-Christian philosophy of Nazism and followed by an era of unimaginable mass murders in the name of the atheistic philosophy of Communism.

*

Pinker comes across as liberal in the best sense of the word. But there are hints in his philosophy that Pera is correct and that human rights need something more than Pinker's hyper-rationalism to sustain them. *Enlightenment Now*'s materialistic defense of democracy is weak. Overall, and over time, freedom can make us happy and rich, it's true. But what if for a while it doesn't? What if it needs to be defended through war or economic collapse? Once the sacred status of liberty is lost, will mothers send their sons to die for a generally upward trend on a statistical graph?

And then there's Pinker's frequent praise of "moral realist" philosopher Peter Singer, whose defense of infanticidal euthanasia is both poorly reasoned and morally barbaric. The ugly truth is: we can live quite happily in a world of scientific miracles even as we transform ourselves into monsters. Various agencies estimate there are 40-50 million abortions worldwide every year. If each of these represents the purposeful and unjustified taking of a human life, then all our medical, technological, economic, and cultural comforts are merely a moral anesthesia easing our descent into savagery.

*

But for a glimpse of how the Enlightenment Narrative's embrace of pure reason can undermine the very foundations of the Western civilization that created it, you have to turn to Israeli historian Yuval Noah Harari's bestseller *Sapiens: A Brief History of Humankind.* Though full of quirky insights and interesting information, it is a textbook example of how materialistic logic can lead to philosophical pathology.

Harari's central contention is that the "ability to speak about fictions is the most unique feature of Sapiens language." He goes on to say that "fiction has enabled us not merely to imagine things, but to do so collectively," by creating what he calls an "inter-subjective reality," or "inter-subjective order existing in the shared imagination of ... millions of people" and thus allowing them to work together in ways other animals can't.

"Inter-subjective phenomena are neither malevolent frauds nor insignificant charades. They exist in a different way from physical phenomena such as radioactivity, but their impact on the world may still be enormous."

Among the fictions that create these inter-subjective phenomena, according to Harari, are religion, nationhood, money, law and human rights.

"None of these things exists outside the stories that people invent and tell one another. There are no gods in the universe, no nations, no money, no human rights, no laws, and no justice outside the common imagination of human beings."

Now here is an area where I can speak with some expertise. I am a lifelong maker of fiction and I am here to tell you: this is not what fiction is; this is not how fiction works. Good fiction does not create phenomena, it describes them. Like all art, fiction is a language for communicating a type of reality that can't be communicated in any other way: the interplay of human consciousness with itself and the world. That experience can be delusional, as when we hear voices, mistake infatuation for love, or convince ourselves that slavery is moral. But the very fact that it can be delusional points to the fact that it can be healthy and accurate as well. When it is healthy, the "common imagination of human beings," can be regarded as an organ of perception, like the eye. Fiction merely describes the world of morality and meaning which that organ perceives.

Because Harari does not believe this world of moral meaning exists, he thinks it is created by the fiction rather than the other way around. For example, he refers to women as sapiens "possessing wombs," and declares that only "the myths of her society assign her unique feminine roles" like raising children. No one who has ever met a woman outside the planet Vulcan can imagine this politically correct nonsense to be the actual case. Harari himself speaks quite tenderly of the maternal feelings of sheep. What myths have the rams been telling the ewes? Different male and female roles are a human universal because womanhood is a complete inner reality. Myths describe it truly or falsely; they don't make it what it is.

Harari can imagine the "complex emotional worlds" of cows. He believes that the existence of these worlds creates an obligation in us to treat cows more kindly than we currently do. Fair enough. But why then can he not deduce the reality of human rights, natural law, economic value, and femininity from the far more complex inner experience of humans?

"Human rights are a fictional story just like God and heaven," Harari told an interviewer. "They are not a biological reality. Biologically speaking, humans don't have rights."

This language may not necessarily be malign. It may not suggest Harari has no visceral respect for human rights. But it does not inspire confidence in his ultimate commitment to those rights either. It is not exactly "Give me liberty or give me death!" In fact, Harari has argued that increasing information may require increasing centralization of power, the old progressive canard that the world has become too complex for individual freedom and must now be run by experts. This sort of thing makes one suspicious that Harari — that such reason-worshipping thinkers in general — are living justifications for Marcello Pera's fears that freedom cannot defend itself without specifically Judeo-Christian faith.

*

It is the Enlightenment Narrative that creates this worship of reason, not reason itself. In fact, most of the scientific arguments against the existence of God are circular, self-proving, and just plain bad. They pit advanced scientific thinkers against simple, literalist religious believers. They dismiss error and mischief committed in the name of science — the Holocaust, atom bombs, climate change — but amberize error and mischief committed in the name of faith — "the Crusades, the Inquisition, witch hunts, the European wars of religion," as Pinker has it.

And by assuming the spiritual realm is a fantasy, they irrationally dismiss our experience of it. Our brains perceive the smell of coffee, yet no one argues coffee isn't real. But when the same brain perceives the immaterial — morality, the self, or God — it is presumed to be spinning fantasies. Coming from those who worship reason, this is lousy reasoning.

*

The point of this essay is not to argue the truth of Christianity. I argue only this: the modern intellectual's difficulty in believing is largely an effect created by the overwhelming dominance of the Enlightenment Narrative, and that narrative is simplistic and incomplete.

Did we, for example, *escape* Christianity into science? From Roger Bacon to Galileo to Newton, the men who sparked the scientific revolution were all believing Christians. Doesn't this make it seem plausible that — despite the church's occasional interference — modern science was actually an outgrowth of Christian thought?

And is science still moving away from that Christian outlook, or has its trajectory begun to turn? It may have once seemed reasonable to assume the clockwork world uncovered by Isaac Newton would inexorably lead us to atheism, but those clockwork certainties have themselves dissolved as science advanced. Quantum physics has raised mind-boggling questions about the role of consciousness in the creation of reality. And the virtual impossibility of an accidental universe precisely fine-tuned to the maintenance of life has scientists scrambling for "reasonable" explanations.

Some (like Pinker) try to explain these mysteries away. For example, they've concocted a wholly unprovable theory that we are in a multiverse. There are infinite universes, they say, and this one just happens to be the one that acts as if it were spoken into being by a gigantic invisible Jew! Others bruit about the idea that we live in a computer simulation — which is a tacit admission of faith, though it may be faith in a god who looks like the nerd you beat up in high school.

In any case, scientists used to accuse religious people of inventing a "God of the Gaps," i.e. using religion to explain away what science had not yet uncovered. But multiverses and simulations seem very much like a Science of the Gaps, jerry-rigged nothings designed to circumvent the simplest explanation for the reality we know.

*

Pinker credits Kant with naming the Enlightenment Age, but ironically, it is Kant who provided a plausible foundation for the faith that he believed was the only guarantor of morality. His *Critique of Pure Reason* proposed an update of Plato's form theory, positing that the phenomenal world we see and understand is but the emanation of a noumenal world of things-as-they-are, an immaterial plane we cannot fully know.

In this scenario, we can think of all material existence as a sort of language that imperfectly expresses an idea. Every aspect of language is physical: the brain sparks, the tongue moves, the air is stirred, the ear hears. But the idea expressed by that language has no physical existence whatsoever. It simply is. And whether the idea is "two plus two equal four" or "I love you," or "slavery is wrong," it is true or false whether or not we perceive the truth or falsehood of it.

This, as I see it, is the very essence of Christianity. It is the religion of the Word. The model, of course, is Jesus, the perfect Word that is the thing itself. But each of us are made in that image, continually expressing in flesh some aspect of the maker's mind.

This is why Jesus speaks in parables, not just to communicate their meaning, but also to assert the validity of their mechanism. In the very act of understanding a parable, we are forced to acknowledge that physical interactions — the welcoming home of a prodigal son, say — speak to us about immaterial things like love and forgiveness. As with parables, so with all life: the physical *is* the spiritual as the bread and wine are the body and blood, which is God.

To acknowledge that our lives are parables for spiritual truths may necessitate a belief in the extraordinary, but it is how we all live whether we confess that belief or not. We all know the words "two plus two" express the human version of a truth that is both immaterial and universal. We likewise know we are not just flesh-bags of chemicals, but that our bodies imperfectly express the idea of ourselves. We know that whether we strangle a child or give a beggar bread, we take physical actions that convey moral meaning. We know this morality does not change when we don't perceive it. In ancient civilizations, where everyone, including slaves, considered slavery moral, it was immoral still. They simply hadn't discovered that truth yet, just as they hadn't figured out how to make an automobile, though all the materials and principles were there.

We live in this world of morality and meaning — right up until the moment it causes us pain or guilt or shame or gets in the way of our ambitions or happiness. Then suddenly we look at the only logical source of the meaning we perceive and say, "I do not know Him."

Understood in this way, there is no barrier of ignorance between Christian faith and science. Rather, the faith that made the West can still defend it from the dual threat of regressive religion and barbaric scientism. In fact, it may be the only thing that can.

*

A West whose ethicists coolly contemplate infant euthanasia, whose nations roll back their magnificent jurisprudence to make room for the atrocity of Sharia, whose historians argue themselves out of the objective reality of human rights because they have lost faith in the numinous basis of those rights — such a West may not be *heading* for disaster. It may be smack in the midst of a comfortable and prosperous disaster to which our default atheism makes us blind, a science fiction-style dystopia in which we are increasingly happy and increasingly savage at the same time.

It need not be so. Outside of the Enlightenment Narrative, there is absolutely no reason to abandon the faith that created our civilization. The flowering of the Western mind took place under the Christian sun. The light that led us here can lead us on.

Can We Be Silent In A World Gone Mad?

THE 2019 PULLIAM DISTINGUISHED FELLOW IN JOURNALISM ADDRESS AT HILLSDALE COLLEGE

April 9, 2019

There's something about human corruption that has always struck me as comical. This is not, as my wife has reminded me more than once, my most attractive personality trait and I can even see where it might strike some as a bit disturbing. To laugh at a politician who peddles his influence, or a policeman who's on the payroll of the mob is the sort of behavior one expects to find only in Hell or Chicago — and it's possible one day I will end up in one or the other.

But in my defense, corruption almost always contains an element of the absurd. It is as if the human mind transforms itself into the age-old parody of a dishonest philosopher who makes "the worse appear the better cause." Wherever human corruption occurs, there always seems to have been a moment when the perpetrator decided that wreaking havoc on his neighbor, or his country, or his own soul, or all three was really a pretty fine idea. Edgar Allen Poe called this preposterous human tendency toward mayhem the "Imp of the Perverse."

As an example, consider the recent scandal in which more than thirty wealthy elites were indicted for bribing, lying, and cheating to win their children acceptance into top-notch universities. They had their perfectly healthy offspring diagnosed with learning disabilities so they could game the entry exams. They photoshopped their kids' faces onto the bodies of athletes and then paid off college athletic directors to recommend them for acceptance. The ancient rationale for the existence of an aristocracy was that the privileged classes, freed from the necessity of labor and trade, had the leisure to refine their moral and aesthetic senses. And yet these members of our American aristocracy, who should have had moral sense coming out of their ears, instead must have thought to themselves, "Here's a fine idea! I will model for my children the art of clownish dishonesty. I will train them to wallow in the personal degradation of mindless ambition and humiliating deception. I will ensure that their academic achievements will be devoid of pride, their reputations will be based on lies, and their consciences will be blackened with shame, or depraved with rationalization. And this will make me a good parent."

That shouldn't strike me as funny, but it does. Because it is. In fact, it's the oldest joke in the world. It's the joke about the guy in a tuxedo who falls in a mud puddle, or the snooty society doyenne who gets a custard pie smack in the kisser. It's funny because they're supposed to be one thing, a high and admirable thing, and instead, to our surprise, they become another thing, low and ridiculous.

And when I say that's the oldest joke in the world, I'm not exaggerating even a little, because it's the joke of the human condition itself. You may have heard the one about the man and woman in the Garden of Paradise. Everything perfect and nothing to do but make love to one another and walk with God. Only one rule — only one. And yet somewhere along the line, the Imp of the Perverse whispered in their ears, the worse appeared the better cause, and the thought occurred to them: "Here's a fine idea…" They — we — were created to be one thing, a high and admirable thing, and instead, to our surprise, we are another, low and ridiculous.

What makes us uncomfortable about laughing at this is the extent of the catastrophe. There is an echo of the Fall of Man in every act of evil. Once corruption turns to violence — and it very often does — all the comedy goes out of it. And yet the absurdity remains. Whether it's a lone gunman who slaughters people at their prayers, or an entire civilization that immolates itself in mass murder and world war, there's always a moment when someone, indeed maybe everyone, thinks to himself: "This is a fine idea!"

"To do evil, a human being must first of all believe that what he's doing is good or else that it's a well-considered act in conformity with natural law." So wrote Alexander Solzhenitsyn in *The Gulag Archipelago*, his magisterial description of Soviet Communism's terrors and tortures and prisons. Solzhenitsyn was taking issue with the Shakespearean notion of evildoers who know themselves for the bad guys they are: Richard III, for instance, who declared he was, "determined to prove a villain," or Aaron the Moor who wanted to have "his soul black like his face."

Solzhenitsyn notes that Shakespeare's self-aware villains are amateurs at the art of murder. They "stopped short at a dozen corpses," he said, "because they had no ideology."

"Ideology," he writes, "is what gives evildoing its long-sought justification and gives the evildoer the necessary steadfastness and determination. That is the social theory which helps to make his acts seem good instead of bad in his own and others' eyes ..."

I believe, even by his own logic, Solzhenitsyn is only half right — or at least only states half the case. And he sells old Shakespeare short.

He is right about this: an ideology — a bad ideology — is the vehicle by which the fine idea of corruption can spread over an entire society like a fog. In the impenetrable murk of a bad ideology, the corruption becomes all-but-invisible until even the best and the brightest can engage in the most appalling behavior completely unawares.

Take, for example, the case of George Washington. How else but in the fog of a bad ideology could so great and virtuous a champion of liberty not only hold chattel slaves but find their desire for freedom incomprehensible? Here was the man who, with a victorious army at his command and the support of the people at his back, refused a continental kingdom for love of liberty. For love of liberty, he handed his sword and his commission over to the civilian authorities. With that one action, for love of liberty, he gave Liberty itself "a local habitation and a name": the United States of America. And yet, writes his biographer Ron Chernow, Washington "suffered from a conceptual blind spot about slavery, tending to regard it as a fair economic exchange." Until time and experience gave the great man greater wisdom toward the end of his life, Washington literally could not understand why his slaves wouldn't work his land as diligently as he did, or why they would try to escape when he had treated them so well. He, of all men, could not see that they acted for love of liberty. He was lost in the fog of the bad ideology of chattel slavery into which he'd been born.

The same phenomenon occurs today when otherwise true-hearted and moral women commit abortion. The child's individual and irreplaceable DNA proves the fetus is not the woman's body and that therefore whether it lives or dies is not her choice. Our amazing new ability to see life within the womb reveals the baby's obvious humanity and capacity to suffer. And yet in the fog of a bad ideology, even sophisticated, educated, ethically conscious women with the means to provide the child some path to certain survival, feel justified in doing the thing they do.

When the fog of corruption is widespread and thick enough, its blinding effects appear in the smallest everyday actions. Not long ago, I took Ubers to and from a restaurant in Los Angeles. In both cars, the drivers, a young man in one direction and a young woman in the other, were playing rap music at full volume. Rather than ask them to turn it off, I decided to take the opportunity to listen and, by chance or providence, I heard the same song in both directions. Using the foulest possible language, the rapper referred to women in disgusting and dehumanizing terms and laughed and bragged about how he had abused and humiliated one woman through forced sex and violence.

It occurred to me as I rode along that these Uber drivers were probably very nice young people. Maybe they remembered to call their mothers on Sunday. Maybe their friends could count on them in times of trouble and so on. And yet, not only did they seem to feel no compunction about grooving to violent pornography while on the job, they seemed to think the elderly gentleman in the back seat — the customer who would determine their star ratings and the sizes of their tips — might also enjoy a bit of musical rape and human degradation, or at least find in it no cause to complain. Until I arrived at my destinations, I was fully immersed in an atmosphere of moral madness.

The existence of this atmosphere changes our sense of individual responsibility. Despite the fact that he participated in the evil of chattel slavery, we honor George Washington as a great man — and rightly so. We may be appalled by the act of abortion, but we're shocked if even an anti-abortion crusader suggests that the decent women who kill their unborn babies should be imprisoned. And if I had dragged one of my Uber drivers out from behind the wheel and given him or her a stern talking-to about what a decent song lyric sounds like, I would have earned the description of me that appeared recently in the magazine *Vanity Fair* when they called me, "an old crank."

To live in a state of moral madness is to live in a kind of ignorance — ignorance in the Platonic-Aristotelian sense, as when Aristotle says, "Every wicked person acts in ignorance of the things he ought to do and avoid." In this widespread atmosphere of ethical insanity, even those who dissent often can no longer fully experience the absurdity and horror of what's happening around them. It wasn't villains or gangsters who called for the crucifixion of Christ. It was the good people, the religious leaders, the guardians of morality, and the decent, ordinary men and women on the street: you and me. Even those who had recognized Jesus as the messiah days before at best stood by and watched as the wretched thing was done. We have it on good authority that they knew not what they did.

But just how deep does this ignorance go? How complete is it? The slaveholder or the aborting mother or the youngster tapping his toes to tunes of rape and savagery — are they really wholly unaware that they are acting wrongly, that they have, at least temporarily, lost their moral minds? To be sure, a person can become so depraved his conscience dies, but can everyone, everywhere, forever sin in blissful ignorance?

I don't believe they can. That's not what the evidence suggests.

This is what I meant when I said that Solzhenitsyn's statement is only half true by his own logic. He says that "to do evil a human being must first of all believe that what he's doing is good." But this implies that humans instinctively know there are such things as good and evil and have an inborn sense of what it takes to create a moral justification that transforms one into the other. After all, no one ever had to devise an ideology to justify kindness or charity or love.

This is the place where I should point out that science confirms, to some degree, that we are inherently moral beings. Experiments at the Yale Infant Cognition Center show that even six-month-old babies

23

prefer helpful actions to hindering actions: we're born with a moral sense, or at least develop one very early on. But to be honest, as I'll explain later, I'm not very impressed with these experiments. It may be a sort of blasphemy to say this in the 21st century, but I'm virtually certain that Jesus, Aristotle, and Shakespeare had a more accurate and holistic mental image of humanity than our current psychologists.

So let's go back to Shakespeare. As Solzhenitsyn points out, many of his villains don't take the trouble to convince themselves they're doing good. They act, in the words of St. Augustine, with "no inducement to evil but evil itself." Some, like Aaron the Moor and Iago, are irredeemably beyond remorse. But many of the Bard's most prolific murderers are brought low by a moral force that seems to come from both within them and without. Richard III may be "determined to prove a villain," but the ghosts of his victims return to him on Bosworth Field and demand that he remember his atrocities, "despair and die." Lady Macbeth prays to the spirits to fill her heart with the "direst cruelty," but she then executes herself because she can't wash the visionary blood off her hands. Perhaps most profoundly, Macbeth himself, having slaughtered his way to the throne of Scotland, comes to understand that, in doing so, he has stepped out of the meaning of life into "a tale told by an idiot, full of sound and fury, signifying nothing."

In other words, some of Shakespeare's worst villains not only fall afoul of conscience but conscience is conceived of as an organ of perception that sees a moral reality that actually exists, if only in the interplay between man's mind and the mysterious world-as-it-is. To put this more simply, Shakespeare's villains feel guilty because they are guilty. They know right from wrong because there is right and wrong and mankind is created in such a way that we can tell the difference. We can't stop knowing even when our fallen humanity is moved to do evil.

I believe the evidence for the truth of Shakespeare's vision is found not just on stage but everywhere around us. Again and again, we see unmistakable signs that people who do evil, even after convincing themselves that evil is good, are tormented by the two-headed fury of conscience and moral reality. Even in a world gone mad, where everyone around them is convinced that the worse is the better cause, they know the truth and suffer from the knowledge.

Look at the way they behave. People who defend evil ideologies justify themselves with constant expectations of catastrophe as if we were in an endless state of war-like emergency that required the suspension of moral order. People who defend evil ideologies stifle dissent, as if even a mention of their error will force them to face the truth of it. And they reliably stumble from smaller sins into greater and greater atrocities as if they hope to escape to some level of complete depravity at which their wickedness will finally seem sanctified to them.

Read the diaries of the American slaveholders. They were obsessively afraid that their slaves would rise up and murder them in their beds. The phrase "murdered in our beds," is almost a constant refrain with them. Does that suggest to you a quiet conscience?

Or return to the Soviets and their gulags. If they were fully convinced that the Communist Party was the source of all goodness, why were they so desperate to crush any disagreement? Why did they see dissent everywhere, even where there was none? They imprisoned, tortured and executed people not just for the slightest aberration from Communist ideology, but for the possibility that aberration might one day occur. Do men who are certain of their moral position behave that way? Or is it only those whose sense of virtue depends on a shared delusion so fragile that even the possibility of clarity will shatter it?

Finally, consider a vote in the American Senate just last February. A bill that would have strengthened the penalties for denying care to babies born alive after an attempted abortion was scuttled by forty-four senators who support abortion. Less than a quarter century after such supporters told us abortion should be "safe, legal and rare," their activists are encouraging women to "shout their abortions" with pride and their lawmakers cast votes that deny protections to fully born babies. If a baby fully born is not a human being with a right to life, who the hell is? But of course, if you have taken a step down the road to evil, you're forced to run farther and farther down that road lest you stop and turn and see yourself as you are.

Whether they act with "no inducement to evil but evil itself," or justify their acts with ideology, those who do wrong feel guilty because they are guilty, and they act that way. They see catastrophe looming everywhere. They stifle dissent. They escape from smaller sins into greater and greater atrocities. They have distorted the moral universe and their own souls. They are living in a world gone mad.

Christians believe that this madness is, to some degree, intrinsic to our situation. That could almost serve as a definition of original sin. If nothing else, this theory acts as a corrective to nostalgia, the temptation to believe that life was far better and more moral in the good old days. Recently, I was discussing a Platonic dialogue with my son Spencer, a brilliant classical scholar trained at Yale and Oxford. Reflecting on the convulsions of outrage and dialectal savagery on social media, I told Spencer I yearned for that more civilized world of ancient Athens where a great philosopher like Socrates could spend his days discussing ideas with his pals in the agora. After a brief, embarrassed silence, my son said quietly, "Dad — they killed Socrates." So much for the good old days.

Indeed, before these times of rampant abortion and rap music, there were days when people were set on by police dogs and lynch mobs for the crime of having brown skin. There were holocausts and slavery and war. There always are. The fog of insanity thins and gathers, hangs offshore and comes rolling in, but there is always moral madness somewhere and there is always someone who will call it justice.

Still, as the great philosopher Gandalf the Wizard told Frodo: "We have to decide what to do with the time that is given us." We have to determine how to behave when our era, when our corner of the world, goes insane.

To reach, as I have, the age of Gandalf, is to see the world as from a height: you lose touch with life on the ground a little, but you gain perspective. I look around at the United States and I see a nation full of wonders. Longer life in better health than ever before. Running water everywhere. Plentiful and inexpensive food. All information, literature, and art available at the touch of a pocket-size phone. Most of the crises we face are crises of the imagination. If, when reading the news, you edit out all the stories about the disasters some gloomy experts think might happen, you'll be amazed at just how terrific things are here. To paraphrase the immortal lyrics of Johnny Mercer in the only lousy song he ever wrote: for Americans, everything truly is tickety-boo.

I attribute this astounding liberation from humankind's long history of poverty, plague, and violence to three developments: science, capitalism, and liberalism, by which last I mean the commitment to self-government and individual human rights. It's my personal theory that these three innovations spring from one idea: the idea that all creation is made to work in freedom without intrusive overseers. That is the thought that links Isaac Newton to Adam Smith to the American founding fathers. Science, capitalism, and liberalism all assume that the proper machinery is in place and does not need to be micro-managed by the authorities. God doesn't need to tinker with the stars; He made them to do the starry stuff they do. Governments don't need to control the economy; if we trade with each other under a few reasonable rules of fairness, our ambition and creativity will cause everyone to rise and thrive. And individuals don't require monarchs to dictate their actions, thoughts, and speech. We have been given the moral wherewithal to run our own homes, communities, and countries ourselves.

In this three-in-one trinity of ideas, we have become uniquely blessed. But in defense of those blessings, it's worthwhile to note the patches of fog — of bad ideology — that seem to be gathering in the intellectual centers where the culture of the future is often made. To remind you, the three symptoms I look for are an inordinate fear of catastrophe, the silencing of dissent, and the steady progress from moral error to atrocity.

I find these symptoms beginning to appear, to various degrees of severity, in elite thinking about the economy, race, and sex.

In the realm of the economy, capitalism and improved property rights have cut extreme poverty in half worldwide over the last thirty years, and in America the poor now live at the level of the middle class of the 1980's. Yet a presidential candidate who praised the mass murdering Communists of Cuba and unapologetically honeymooned in the slave state of the Soviet Union preaches socialism to a nodding press and cheering crowds of young people.

In the matter of race relations, surely, there is one, and only one, correct approach: to love your neighbor who is made in God's image, and to judge each person by the content of his character rather than the color of his skin. Yet after my father's generation fought to end the wickedness of segregation and Jim Crow, I see my children's generation attending universities with segregated dorms, where they are taught the viciously racist philosophy of intersectionality as if it were the cure for bigotry rather than a new strain of the old disease.

As for human sexuality, it is always a disordered business, where the most urgent desires of our material bodies and the deepest longings of our fallen souls conjoin. But that there is such a thing as human sexuality, that it is centered on the differences between the two sexes, male and female, that those differences are written into our very cells and are among the chief joys and consolations of experience, and indeed are the very archetype and inspiration of all earthly love and creation — these are human universals, known from the jungle up and essential to the formation of every single society that has ever existed on earth. The idea that these yin-yang bedrock facts of life are merely cultural constructs and can therefore be completely erased by wishing very hard and dressing in one another's clothing is simple lunacy.

In each of these cases, I see exaggerated fear of catastrophe in the form of climate panic, overblown anxiety about fascism and white supremacism, and the anguished, hysterical cowering from debate in so-called safe spaces. I see the silencing of dissent where voices of fact and logic, science and experience are punished in the workplace, edited out of search engines, deplatformed from social media, and barred from campus or met with heckling and violence. And I see the progress from error toward atrocity, from government interference and cronyism in the economy to the certain economic ruin of socialism, from supposedly corrective racial preferences to resurrected segregation and the bigotry of intersectionality, and from the disparagement of femininity and motherhood to infanticide and the sexual butchery of children in the name of gender reassignment.

Like the good ideas that have brought us so far, these bad ideas, to my mind, are all one idea. It is the idea that man is matter, and that therefore the moral world can only be a fictional creation of his brain which can be changed by changing the stories that he is told and is allowed to tell.

I mentioned earlier that I don't entirely trust the modern psychological studies of human morality detailed in books by psychologists like Jonathan Haidt, Paul Bloom, and Steven Pinker. The reason is this. They are based on the idea that human morality is entirely a creation of evolution and nothing more. Consider the logic of that for a minute. Surely, the human sense of sight evolved to see light because in reality there is a phenomenon that can be seen as light. The sense of hearing evolved because in reality there are such phenomena that can be apprehended as sound. Likewise the human sense of morality evolved — does it then follow that morality is entirely our creation, entirely subject to our changing opinions? Are light and sound our creations? No. They are the human experience of things that are there. So it is with morality. Conscience is our human sense of a truth about the universe. The psychologists should have read their Shakespeare.

Let me finish up with an example of how this faulty logic can feed into bad ideology.

In studies of evolved morality, psychologists tell their subjects little stories and ask them to make moral judgements about them. In one of these stories, a loving brother and sister commit an act of incest; they have sex. They're careful the sister doesn't get pregnant. They never repeat the act. And their relationship continues as before. People hear this story and instinctively sense that incest is wrong, but they can't explain why it's wrong in this particular case. From this, some psychologists conclude that the incest taboo is an outmoded evolutionary remnant from the days when the resulting dangerous pregnancies could not be prevented.

But the story itself is based on the false premise that human beings are mere physical objects, that the spiritual relationship between brother and sister has no real being, no inherent nature, and that therefore brother and sister can have sex without violating the core truth of that relationship. In fact, in the story, they have sex without changing their relationship at all, which has never happened to anyone ever — no matter who they were — since the world began.

What the psychologists have really discovered is that the human moral sense evolved to perceive reality, not stupid stories that falsely describe reality. In fact, the subjects instinctively understand the moral universe better than the clever shrinks who wrote the stories. If you've ever wondered why intellectuals seem so incredibly stupid sometimes, that's why.

Now carry this logic over to a more pressing issue like abortion. The moral philosopher Judith Jarvis Thompson wrote a famous paper called "A Defense of Abortion," which includes this now very popular argument: Thompson describes a situation in which you wake up and find yourself next to a famous violinist. The violinist has a fatal kidney condition and your kidneys are now hooked up to his to keep him alive. In nine months, the violinist will recover and then you will be free. Thompson argues that you have the right to unhook yourself from the violinist because he should not be allowed to force you to use your body for his survival. Therefore, you have the right to have an abortion on the same grounds.

Now Thompson is a famous moral philosopher and I'm just a barefoot teller of tales, but that's nuts. For one thing, it sounds like Thompson missed the day in Health class when they explained that you don't just wake up one day and find yourself pregnant; that's not how that works. But more importantly, she conceives of a world in which there is no such thing as motherhood, in which it is not a unique spiritual relationship with a unique set of moral responsibilities. She conceives of the womb as something like a dialysis machine, rather than as a material part of a whole human who exists in a moral universe with which her humanity is interwoven and to which it is bound.

The same materialist illogic applies to socialism, which seeks to solve all human ills with money and thus robs the individual of his work, his ambition, and his charity, of which money is only a symbol. The same illogic applies to intersectionality, which ignores the individual's wisdom, accomplishments, and abilities in order to apportion privileges according to the same racialist principles held by bigots. And the same illogic applies to the attempts to override the yin-yang complementarity of women and men in the name of equality, as if by changing a pronoun or even reshaping a body you could change the nature of the human person that pronoun or body only represents.

The battle for a better world is ultimately not a battle against individuals, but against bad ideas like these that express the absurdly fallen human heart and the Imp of the Perverse. We don't have to tear down George Washington's statue to condemn chattel slavery. We don't have to imprison women to renounce the killing of babies. We don't have to defend immoral capitalists to defend capitalism itself.

"We wrestle not against flesh and blood," says St. Paul, "but against principalities, against powers, against the rulers of the darkness of this world, against spiritual wickedness in high places." We are in a war of ideas, in which we must defend the idea of the human soul, and the moral world in which it has its being, and its rights to life, liberty, and the pursuit of happiness.

We need to mount this defense with logic, with science, with patience, with humor, and with courage. We need to do it, yes, even if they ban us from Twitter and Facebook. We need to do it even when they riot on campus at our speeches. We need to do it even if our professor marks us down and our boss sends us to HR and our sponsor drops our show. And God prevent it should ever come to this, but if at last the truth itself is outlawed, then outlaws we must become, outlaws like Socrates and Jesus and the believers who faced the Roman lions and the patriots who faced the British guns. I don't mean to be melodramatic, but we have to at least embrace the principle that telling the truth about the human condition is worth great sacrifice so we'll be ready to face the lesser sacrifices that, even here, even now, the truth sometimes demands. We have to be ready to make those sacrifices for truth because the wages of lies are corruption, slavery, and death.

This country has been so free, so safe, so powerful so long, that it is easy to forget how quickly freedom can be lost in the fog of bad ideas. Wandering in that fog, the world goes mad, and in a world gone mad, we cannot be silent.

The Art of Making Sense

KEYNOTE ADDRESS TO THE VITAE FOUNDATION

June 6, 2019

I'm actually a little nervous to come before you and speak on a topic that is literally a matter of life and death. As a novelist, I've spent most of my professional life making up stories that never happened about people who don't exist. The excuse I often use on my wife when she can't understand how I could be so clueless about something, or virtually everything, is I tell her: "Hey, I'm just a barefoot teller of tales."

And I really don't know why anyone would listen to the opinions of a person who spends his time doing something so frivolous. It's as if a movie actor were to tell you what he thinks about politics — it's absurd — who ever heard of such a thing.

But the Vitae Foundation is an organization dedicated to sending messages into our country and into our culture about the value of human life, and specifically the life of unborn children. Essentially, they, and all of you who have the wisdom and decency to support them, have taken it upon yourselves to speak out for those who cannot speak for themselves, for the one person in the abortion scenario who has everything to lose and yet no power and no voice with which to influence the situation.

So I thought: If what we're here to do is help Vitae send messages, I might lend a hand by telling you some of the things I've learned from a lifetime of telling stories. I've titled this talk "The Art of Making Sense."

Making sense has been a lifetime obsession of mine, ever since I was a child. There may have been psychological reasons for this or it may have been an inborn trait, I don't know, but ever since I can remember it was my ambition that the things I thought, the things I said, and the things I did would all be coherent — they would all stick together as part of a reasonable whole. When you make sense, you say what you believe and therefore mean what you say and therefore act in accordance with it and therefore you are who you seem to be.

Now, of course, when I say making sense was my ambition, what I mean is that I was not making sense most of the time but wanted to, and many decades of life had to go by before I had any idea how to even begin the attempt. Still, the ambition itself has had a powerful effect on my life.

The other day, I had one of the most extraordinary conversations I've ever had. So deep and heartfelt that it sounded like art, like dialogue from a play or movie. I was sitting in a restaurant with two old friends, two men I've known a long time, both of them a little older than me. (You can only get a *little* older than me, after that ...)

All three of us are men who love women, men who are enchanted by women not as television and movies tell us women are supposed to be, and not as women tell us they are — both of which have very little to do with reality — but we're enchanted with women as we actually experience them. For all three us, the company of women has been one of the centrals joys and consolations of living.

So, after a couple of drinks, we began to talk about committing adultery. One of us had been married several times, and had cheated on two of his wives after the marriage was on the rocks and he and the wife of the moment had drifted apart. In both cases, he came into a situation where the sexual temptation was too much for him and shortly afterward the marriage was over. This was a violation of his own values and he felt very bad about it but in the moment he just couldn't resist.

My other friend married only one woman and loved her and stayed married to her until she died, but sometimes, over the years, he fell in love with other women and he could not bear to let the experience of love pass him by. He said he would not have missed his adulteries for the world. They were part of what made him who he was.

Then there was me. I had my 39th wedding anniversary last week, and I've been rather blissfully faithful. (Which you could have guessed. Otherwise, I wouldn't be telling this story.) And to be fair, my marriage is extraordinary. It's been the sort of lifelong romance that I don't think happens very often.

One of these men asked me how I had resisted the sexual temptations, which were many (I worked in Hollywood), and the other asked me how I had denied myself other possible experiences of love, which were one or two. And I told them it was because, more than sex and more even than new love, more than anything else really in my life, I had always wanted to make sense. I wanted to say what I believed and therefore mean what I say and therefore act in accordance with it and therefore be who I seem to be. To my wife, to my children, to the public, to everyone. I wanted to make sense.

I have lost a good deal to become a person who makes sense, to say what I believed and to be who I seem. I've lost not just chances to commit adultery, but by speaking about my political conservatism I also sacrificed most of a successful Hollywood career, not to mention many friends, and some family and a lot of money. And I can testify, after a great deal of self-examination, that it has been well worth it. I believe that making sense is the most important thing a person or a society can do.

It was the desire to make sense that made me a storyteller in the first place. Like most artists, I was an unhappy kid. And like many unhappy kids, I used to escape into daydreams. And I daydreamed about the usual boy things — having super powers and rescuing girls from danger, being a great fighter and rescuing girls from danger, and having a souped up car and using it to rescue girls from danger. Boys spend a lot of time daydreaming about rescuing girls from danger.

But even as a child, before I would let myself indulge in any daydream, I always had to invent a story that explained why the daydream made sense. How did I get my super powers? (Did I come from another planet? Drink a serum? Benefit from a magic spell?) How did I become such a great fighter? Why was a seven-year-old boy allowed to drive such a souped up car? My explanations didn't have to be realistic. I could make up my own rules. But once I made them up, the rules of the explanation had to be obeyed. The story had to make internal sense. Over time, I became very good at this, I became good at inventing stories that made sense — I became a novelist.

No one thinks about this much, but everyone knows instinctively that a good story has to make internal sense. It has to hang together. How many times have you walked out of a movie or finished a novel and said, no, that was ridiculous, the hero would never have done that, or if the villain was so brilliant how could he make such a ridiculous mistake, or if the president was a complete idiot how could he also be a Russian super spy so cagey no one could find any evidence to prove it after two and a half years? It doesn't make any sense.

The reason we want stories to make sense is because stories are a way of speaking about reality – and reality makes sense. This is a wonderful thing about reality that we don't appreciate enough. When you see something in reality that doesn't make sense it's only because you don't know enough about it. You naturally want to find out more in order to find out what sense it makes.

This is how science advances. For hundreds of years Newton's theories made sense of the motion of the planets, but as our power to observe those movements became more sophisticated, we saw that some of them were out of keeping with Newton's ideas, and so we needed a new theory, the theory of relativity, to make them make sense again.

Because reality makes sense, we know our spiritual beliefs, if they are true, also have to hang together — and that helps us refine our values. If we believe in a good and loving God, for instance, we have to explain why he allows us to commit evil. And if we explain that by saying, well, God wants us to be able to exercise free will, then we have to concede that, if free will is so important to God that He would allow evil, maybe we have to allow one another to exercise free will as much as possible.

Then when we've established our values, our actions have to make sense in light of those values. If we say that God wants us to be free and therefore we must allow for freedom, we can no longer justify the age old practice of human slavery. It's really amazing. We are willing to fight wars over this, to kill and to die, simply to bring our actions into alignment with our values: to make sense of ourselves.

If you start with the right principles, with true ideas, with a loving God and a respect for your neighbor's freedom, then making sense makes us better as individuals and as a society. It's the most important thing we do.

So this brings me full circle back to telling stories. As I said, stories, like all art, are a way of speaking about reality – but primarily they speak about a specific kind of reality that can't be spoken about in any other way except through representation: art speaks about the reality of the internal human experience.

There is no direct way to communicate what it feels like to be self-consciously alive. Ask the most inarticulate athlete after he's won the big game — ask him, "How does it feel, Champ?" He'll soon find that words like *happy* or *exciting* don't convey what he wants to convey. So he'll tell a story to communicate the answer. He'll say: "It's like waking up on Christmas morning," or "I dreamed of this when I was a kid and now that dream came true." That's why we make movies and paint pictures and write songs. It's the only way we know how to share the experience of being human.

This kind of experience is called subjective experience. Some people think that if an experience is subjective, that means it's not real, or at least less real than an objective experience. But that's not right. Our love for one another, our sense of morality, our joy and suffering, our hopes, dreams, ambitions — these exist on earth only within the human heart but they are very real and have real effects on real life.

So we preserve them. We share them. By making art. By telling stories. And when those stories are true — even if they are fictional — they make sense.

Many years ago, when I was in my late twenties, I got into an argument with a friend. Not an argument like a fight. We got into a debate. It was friendly but it was ferocious. Now, like a large number of my dearest friends over the years, this friend was a Roman Catholic. And I hope there are no Roman Catholics here because I can share with you that these people are the biggest pains in the neck you ever want to meet.

The reason is, since they get a lot of their arguments from a church that's been around for over two thousand years, they've had a lot of time to work out their ideas and a lot of what they say makes sense, which makes it very hard to argue with them. Every now and again, I think one of my Catholic friends is incorrect, but that usually makes one of us.

Anyway, my wife and I had just had our first child, our daughter, and when I saw my daughter being born I had the one and only truly mystical experience of my life. At the moment my daughter came into the world — at the moment I saw a new life emerge in the midst of so much matter — I experienced such intense love that my self broke the bonds of my body and I flowed into the self of my wife and with her into the self of my child and then with them both into a greater self which I experienced as an infinitely vast ocean of love. This lasted less than a second – and then I panicked. I was afraid I would disappear in that ocean. And I yanked myself back into my body. But there was no taking that experience back. There was no dismissing it. And indeed, until many years later, when I came to accept the reality of God, it was an experience of which I could not make sense.

But I think, looking back, this must have disturbed me in ways I didn't quite understand.

Back then, I was very committed to a woman's right to abort her child. I was then, and I am to this today, a natural libertarian. It's my personality, an artist's personality. I want to make my own decisions and I respect your right to make yours. As long as you don't hurt anyone or frighten the horses.

It seemed to me the right to an abortion was an important facet of a woman's right to live life as she wished. Her right to control what happened to her own body. Her right to control her own economic destiny. Her right to have sex when she pleased without being burdened with the responsibility for a new life – "punished with a baby," as Barack Obama once said.

And, there was also the fact that I had not lived a chaste life before my marriage. More than once I had heard those amazingly bracing words, "I'm late." So abortion also seemed necessary in order to protect the future and the ambitions of the most important person in my life: namely myself.

But of course, in order to believe in the right to an abortion, you have to believe that an unborn child is not a human being. After all, there are lots and lots of problems in life, lots of inequalities between peoples, lots of unfairness built into the nature of things. And while we can all appreciate that this causes problems, we also know you're not allowed to solve your problems by killing innocent people.

To me, even way back then, the humanity or non-humanity of the unborn child was the only relevant question. Everything else is a distraction. I've heard people say it's not fair that a woman's body should be hijacked by a fetal parasite. Maybe so, but you can't solve the problem by killing an innocent person. I've heard people talk about the unfairness of pregnancy caused by abuse, rape, incest. No doubt. But you can't solve the problem by killing an innocent person. Lately I've heard people go into long descriptions of how much thought and effort a woman puts into the decision whether to abort. That's not always true by the way, but even if it is, I hear that and think: Well, so what? If I said to you, "Yes, I killed my wife, but I put a lot of thought into it before going ahead," would that make any difference? You can't solve your problems by killing innocent people.

So, as I say, I think the mystical connection I felt with my daughter at the moment of her birth disturbed me with its implications. It disturbed me unconsciously. I didn't want to admit it. But the reason I know it did disturb me is because, one night not long after my daughter's birth, while drinking beers with this devoutly Roman Catholic friend whom I respected very deeply, I brought up my support for abortion, knowing it would mean an argument. In other words, I think I had to hear myself make my case with someone who was capable of arguing back.

And we got into it. I think we must have gone back and forth until well after two o'clock in the morning. And this betokened real commitment on his part, because I only had one kid to wake up for, but being a Catholic, he already had, like, seventeen of them. (This guy, when he takes pictures of his family nowadays, he has to switch the camera to panorama mode.)

So we went back and forth, back and forth. I wasn't religious then, so my friend had no access to arguments about the soul or the Ten Commandments or anything supernatural. He had to stick to pure physical science and logic. And I brought up all the arguments I knew: about the fetus's lack of capacity to suffer, or how it wasn't human because it couldn't make choices or experience self-consciousness —

all the brilliant sophistical maneuvers that will get you a job teaching ethics at Princeton University.

But his argument came down to this: From conception, the fetus had its own DNA — the central marker of physical individuality — so it was not, as the pro-abortionists say, the mother's body. It had a body of its own. And, in time, if no one did anything, if the fetus was simply left alone, it would develop into the person that DNA described. In other words, even if that zygote couldn't feel or think or experience, it was a human being in a moment in time.

And I went to bed that night — stumbled off to bed after drinking all those beers — and I remember to this day lying down and thinking: I lost that argument. He won. I lost. Because we live in time. No one exists outside that dimension. We are, each one of us, a continuum. The successes and failures of my future are traceable back to actions I took in my past. I can't say to you, well, yes, I robbed that bank but that was me yesterday, you can't arrest me for it today. I can argue that I've changed over time, but those changes are the results of things that happened to me and actions I took — repentance, making amends, returning the money I stole — it is I who changed because it is I who live from one day into the next. We celebrated D-Day today. All those old, bent over 90-year-old guys you saw on TV? They're the same 18-year-olds who chased those Nazi bastards back to Berlin.

The great philosopher Clint Eastwood said it best in his brilliant movie *Unforgiven*. His gunfighter character William Munney says: "It's a hell of a thing, killing a man. You take away all he's got and all he's ever gonna have." And so, likewise, you cannot kill an unborn child, even a zygote, without killing the man or woman he or she will become.

The fact was, as I realized that very night or early morning: my friend's philosophy made sense and mine didn't. This is why I hate Roman Catholics.

Now you would think, since I've been telling you about my lifelong commitment to making sense, you would think the moment I realized I had lost the argument I would have risen the morrow morn a new man and entirely changed my mind.

But, of course, I didn't. I didn't change my mind for nearly two decades. Why not? Because, everywhere, the humanity of women spoke to me.

I was surrounded by stories — women's stories — and these stories also made sense. Stories of women who had been raped or were the victims of incest. Stories of women who had aborted children and gone on to live accomplished lives they felt they could not have lived with the child in tow. Stories about women for whom another child would mean poverty and hardship. Stories about all kinds of truly terrible problems that could be solved so very easily by an abortion.

These stories did what stories do: they communicated the inner experience of being a woman in the world, a woman in a jam. And they touched my heart as they were meant to. Because these stories made sense, because they were true stories, they kept me from grasping the nettle of my own broken and nonsensical philosophy. There was one more step I had to take before I could bring myself into alignment with what I knew made sense. I had to begin to hear the stories that were not being told, that *could* not be told.

Because, of course, the unborn child can't tell his story. That's the one person in the abortion event who cannot say a word. The unborn son can't tell you about the times he would have laughed, or the cans he would have kicked down the road on a summer afternoon, or what he would have felt like when he fell in love the first time. The unborn daughter can't tell you what dreams she might have dreamed, or songs she might have sung when sitting by herself, or what child she might have made and loved if only given the chance. They can't tell you they would have been baseball players or opera singers or inventers or scientists — or that maybe they only would have imagined being those things and taken pleasure in it — because that's part of life too. They can't tell you that, yes, they might have been damaged in some way and they might have suffered, but they would have experienced moments of love or joy that flew in the face of that suffering and made their life not only a triumph but an inspiration.

Every unborn child has such a story. And because we live in time, those stories are true whether we allow them to be lived out in fullness or not.

And when you think about it, nearly everything our friends on the other side of this debate do is intended to silence the stories of the unborn. They call an unborn baby a fetus instead of a baby to keep our imaginations from turning to what a baby is, the potential it has, the possibilities.

When pro-life marchers hold up pictures of children in the womb, the abortion defenders attack them, tear them down, tear them up, to keep you, and maybe themselves, from experiencing the child's humanity. NPR has a new style sheet that says a baby is not a baby until it's born. The other day the *New York Times*, a former newspaper, when reporting on a so-called heartbeat bill, described the unborn child's heartbeat as "embryonic pulsing." That's how desperate they are to keep the secret of the child's humanity.

Recently I was hired to write the screenplay to a movie called *Gosnell*, a true story about an abortion doctor who was arrested after years of murdering children fully delivered from the womb. For years, this psychopath had operated under the eyes of the authorities who did not want to do anything that would jeopardize a woman's right to an abortion. They ignored a paper tower of complaints in order to allow this monster to keep doing what he did.

And when the police finally stumbled onto the truth while investigating a prescription drug scam, and when the doctor was finally brought to trial — the most prolific serial killer in American history — the press box in the courtroom was empty. No one would cover it — until Kirsten Powers wrote a column about it at *USA Today* and shamed them into it. The authorities and the press did not want Gosnell's story to get in the way of the pro-abortion story. They didn't want anyone to realize that the pro-abortion story simply doesn't make sense.

When we were researching the film, we spoke to the prosecutor, and she told us that when she interviewed jurors during *voir dire*, the men refused to express an opinion about abortion. That's for a woman to decide, they all said, as if half the country were not allowed to have an opinion about the slaughter of millions of males and females both. The effort to keep people silent, to keep the baby's story from being told has been prodigious. And, up till very recently, it has been more or less successful.

Before I sat down to write the *Gosnell* screenplay, the Pulitzer-Prize-winning political cartoonist Michael Ramirez sent me a copy of one of his drawings. It showed Gosnell's victims, the babies, in the striped outfits of holocaust victims in an Auschwitz-like setting. The caption read: "Never Again."

I hung a copy of the cartoon above my desk and looked at it often as I wrote. I had nightmares every night because I felt the burden of all those lives, of all those stories that would never be lived and never be told.

That burden is on all of us: to tell those stories. To stand up and speak up despite the social pressure, and the dishonest misuse of language, and the violent counter-demonstrations, and the name calling — despite the whole apparatus of silence that has been constructed to shroud the tale each life could tell if it were lived.

This is a great country, with a great founding philosophy, the idea that each of us is endowed by our sovereign God with the right to life, liberty, and the pursuit of happiness. We can't make sense of that philosophy, we can't make sense of ourselves, if we deprive the least of us of the rights granted to them by their Creator and recognized in our founding and cherished in our own hearts.

This organization is committed to that mission, the simple mission of speaking the truth about those who cannot speak it for themselves, I hope God will bless it and you will support it.

We say all of us have the right to life. If we are saying what we believe, then we must mean what we say and act in accordance with it and be the America we seem to be.

We live in time. Our right to the life ahead of us begins when we begin. Nothing else makes sense.

Speaking Across the Abyss: Building Culture in an Age of Unbelief

ACTON INSTITUTE ANNUAL DINNER KEYNOTE ADDRESS

October 15, 2019

It's a genuine honor to be here. I've been a great fan of the Acton Institute for a long time. If there's anyone here who's a regular listener to my podcast, you may well have heard me read a quote from Lord Acton that begins, "At all times, sincere friends of freedom have been rare." It's good to be at a gathering of those sincere friends.

As a novelist, I'm always on the lookout for some metaphor or symbol that will neatly communicate an intriguing truth about the human condition and the age we're living in. One metaphor that frequently comes to my mind these days is the self-curating information app. I have several of these on my iPhone and iPad. They're those gizmos that somehow track the articles you read so they can offer you more of what you like.

Part of what fascinates me about these things is that, like a lot of digital innovations — like internet porn, for instance, or time wasting online games — self-curating information apps seem to have been invented not to solve a problem or make life easier but to exacerbate a human foible, to make one of our flaws even worse. It's as if the inventor had said to himself, "Yes, all men have fallen short of the glory of God, but not as far as they'll be able to fall with my amazing new app!"

The self-curating information app seems programmed to facilitate what the shrinks call confirmation bias, our tendency to process and analyze information in such a way that it supports our preexisting convictions.

My self-curating information apps select articles for me to read according to my tastes. In doing this, they serve my prejudices and gradually eliminate from my news feed any facts or ideas that might disturb my self-certainty or undermine my preconceived notions. Many times — and I'm not making this up, this has happened to me quite a lot — I will open the app to find it filled with articles written by me. I have essentially been reduced to ranting at myself, like one of those poor schizophrenic guys you see on the street sometimes, who are shouting into a cell phone that has been broken for months.

It's no original insight to say that we live in a niche culture. We are each of us increasingly immersed in our own little world of self-confirming ideas. If Jean Paul Sartre was right and "Hell is other people," we should all feel that each of us is living in a sweet solitary heaven of his own. But, of course, Jean Paul Sartre was never right about anything — that's how you become a famous French philosopher.

And I don't think we've begun to come to terms with what a disaster this culture of intellectual isolation really is. In the mazes of our self-curating information universes, the voices of those who disagree with us can only reach us distorted by the filter of our own convictions. We can hear what they're saying, but we can't imagine why they're saying it. Debate seems impossible. Outreach seems impossible. Even common civility sometimes seems impossible.

This is especially disastrous for those of us in the counter-culture, the cultural minority. I'm speaking, of course, about you and me, those members of the thinking classes who believe in God and the human creature made in His image. Many of us now spend our days in a constant state of flabbergasted consternation at the absolute and utter nonsense that comes out of the mouths of seemingly intelligent people.

Men who are smart enough to tie their own ties, and women mentally capable of doing whatever women do before they finally come out of the bathroom in the morning look into cameras and speak into microphones and with straight faces make statements that they themselves have to know are completely insane. Gender is a social construct and therefore a man who believes he is a woman is a woman in fact. Abortion moments before birth, even sometimes after birth — the killing of a newborn baby — is a woman's right, as opposed to a horrific atrocity. All cultures are equally deserving of respect because morality is relative.

Not only are these statements absurd on the face of it, but in spite of that, or possibly because of that, they have come to be protected by an increasingly elaborate system of customs and manners that is enforced by societal sanction. On any given day, you can wake up to find that what human beings have known to be true for thousands of years has suddenly become unspeakable, and if you don't sign on to believing the new lie, you are a bigot, a sexist, a homophobe, some kind of hater, and must be punished. To say that men and women are inherently different, or that transgender women are not women at all, or that an actual real-live woman has exactly zero moral right to terminate the life inside her, or that some savage and oppressive culture is self-evidently inferior to our own — all of these obviously true statements can get you banned from, or bullied on, your social media platform, excoriated in the press, or even fired from your job.

Let me give you one recent example that I think is illustrative of the greater point I'm going to make. In England, a Christian doctor was fired from a department of the National Health Service for refusing to accept the idea that a man who says he's a woman is a woman. The idea offended him both as a scientist and as a Christian.

45

When he appealed his firing, the court ruled against him. The judge wrote that belief in Genesis Chapter One, verse 27, is "Incompatible with human dignity."

Genesis 1:27 reads, "God created man in his image, in the image of God created He him; male and female, created He them." The Imago Dei, the source of our idea of human dignity, the reason we believe that human beings have dignity, was declared by a British court to be incompatible with human dignity — unlike, say, a six-foot-four man with a beard putting a dress on and calling himself Sally.

Where the Imago Dei is deemed out of keeping with human dignity, where the killing of infants is permitted in the name of women's rights, where the butchering of children is encouraged in the name of gender identity, and the silencing of dissent in the name of sensitivity is increasingly approved, the people of God have indeed become strangers in a strange land. We may be forgiven for wondering not merely how we can win back the west's intelligentsia to some semblance of sanity, but how we can communicate with such degraded imbeciles at all. How can we begin to rebuild a culture of truth when we are living in an empire of lies?

I feel my own personal experience offers some hints on how to answer that question. For a long time, I was tangled in the web of some of our mainstream culture's most absurd self-deceptions. I struggled with them constantly in my thought and in my work. As a young man, a modern man, a sophisticated, urban, intellectual man, I was schooled in moral relativism from university upward. It was the intellectual sea in which I swam. The theme of all my early novels was the inescapable subjectivity of human perception, the impossibility of putting your hand or your mind on anything that could reasonably be called reality. All the heroes of my novels were bedeviled by the same questions: How can we ever know what is truly true or whether there is truly truth at all?

I was writing a novel called *True Crime* when I experienced a breakthrough. I was just turning 40 then and was beginning to meditate on mortality. The novel is about a man on death row, which is to say it uses a man on death row as a metaphor for the human condition. In the opening scene, the condemned man awakens from a dream of freedom to find himself inescapably in his cell, undeniably awaiting execution. He reflects that there can be no true confusion between dreams and reality. Death itself draws the dividing line. Death puts a limit on the subjectivity of perception and therefore on the relativity of truth.

That understanding was the beginning of my turn toward faith, my turn toward God. It had been a long, long journey to reach that crossroad.

For most of my life, I was an agnostic, which means, in practice, I was an atheist. I was born and raised a Jew. It was important to my father that my brothers and I were taught the rituals and traditions of the Jewish people. But neither of my parents had any active belief in God. Without God, religious rituals and traditions, wise and beautiful though they may be, seemed nothing but an empty show to me.

I was reluctantly bar mitzvahed by my father's decree, but in the aftermath, I felt like a hypocrite. I had declared myself a living member of a faith but I had no faith because I had been raised to have no faith. One night, when my family was asleep, I crept out of my house, carrying a box full of the jewelry and savings bonds I'd received as bar mitzvah gifts. I buried the box deep in the trash can outside so it would be carted off by the garbage man in the morning before anyone found it. That was my declaration that I was done with the inauthenticity of godless religion.

From then on, through a mentally troubled youth, I was committed to what I and others have called "the burden of unknowing." I continued to carry this burden even when, at 28, I went insane. I became crippled by rage and hypochondria. I was lost in self-aggrandizing fantasies and bizarre mysticism. I yearned for faith but refused to give in to my yearning. I felt it would be weak and cowardly to use God as an imaginary life saver to keep me from drowning in my own misery.

When I look back now, it's painfully obvious to me that God was continually calling out to his tormented child, but I absolutely refused to hear him. I was a modern man, a sophisticated man, an urban, intellectual man — I was, I mean, submerged in the relativistic insanity of modern, sophisticated, urban, intellectual life. To acknowledge my supernatural Creator would have betrayed my integrity as a thinker. I was trapped inside a genuine paradox: for me to accept the truth of God would have been dishonest.

I believe that God, in His mercy, solved this riddle for me. He put aside His majesty for my sake. He even put aside His own name in order to speak to me in secular terms I could understand and accept. Once, using this method, He even pulled me back from the brink of suicide.

I was about 30 then. I was in despair. I was sitting alone in a dark room, plotting my own death. I was repeating over and over in my mind, like a mantra, the words, "I don't know how to live. I don't know how to live."

A baseball game was playing on the radio in the background. A hero of mine, the catcher Gary Carter, hit a ground ball single. After the game, an interviewer asked him how he had managed to beat the throw to first base when his knees had been ruined by squatting in the catcher's position for so many years. Carter was a devout and outspoken Christian. He was always talking to interviewers about Jesus Christ this, or praise Jesus that. I absolutely hated it. Every time he did it, it made me shudder, as if someone had dropped a worm down the back of my shirt. If he had praised Jesus that day, I would have ignored him. But oddly, he didn't mention Christ at all. Instead, as I sat there reciting to myself "I don't know how to live," Carter said simply,

"Sometimes, you just have to play in pain." Those words struck deep into my heart. I seized on them instantly. I thought: "I can do that." And I made the decision to live.

Like all good modern men of that time, I was immersed in the atheistic ideas of Sigmund Freud, and so God sent me a psychiatrist of genius, who healed my mind, and saved my life. It was only then — then when I found mental health and happiness and professional success — when I was no longer afraid that faith would merely be a crutch in troubled times — it was only then I was able to trust myself and to ferret out the flaws in the world's philosophy.

It took me about ten years to work it out. If there is no truth, then it can't be true that there is no truth. If death is real, then life also must be real. And if life is real, then our healthy perceptions of reality, our experience of love and the good, must be at least a human version of the truth and therefore grounded in ultimate truth. In mental health, I could see what I could not see in misery and madness: the logical steps that lead to God, and the human experience of God who is that worm down the back of our shirts, Jesus Christ.

This discovery filled me, and continues to fill me, with so much serenity and joy that I have sometimes gone before God and complained that he allowed me to waste so much of my life before I found him. I have said to him, "Lord, Jew though I am, why did you let me wander in the wilderness for forty years before I came into your promise?" The answer I received was this: God wanted me to make every intellectual error it is possible to make before I stumbled like a gormless idiot on the simple truth. That way, even in jubilant sanity, I would have compassion on an intellectual world mired in so much unnecessary sorrow and pain.

So let me tell you what this experience taught me, because I believe it contains a clue to how we can speak truth into a culture that seems in the grip of increasingly bizarre delusions.

The people who are talking nonsense now — the artists, and the philosophers and commentators and journalists and politicians — the people who say there is no essential difference between men and women, between the blessing of new life and the evil of abortion, between the superiority of free cultures and the inferiority of slave states — these sophisticated people, I mean, who are babbling words of lunatic stupidity, are not just babbling words of lunatic stupidity, they are babbling words of lunatic stupidity that make perfect sense if there is no God.

If there is no ultimate truth, there can be no truth at all. If there is no ultimate good, there can be no good at all. If there is no ultimate love, there can be no love at all, no real spiritual or emotional experience at all. Indeed, if there is no ultimate spirit, there is no spirit whatsoever. Each of us is just a meat puppet with a chemistry set inside.

This materialist outlook is so pervasive now that it affects all of us. Even those of us who have faith treat ourselves like we're meat and chemistry. Listen to the way we talk. When we're excited, we say we're having an adrenaline rush. When we're happy, we say it's a dopamine rush. As if the chemicals caused the emotions, which doesn't even make sense when you think it through. We take medicine for depression as if our spiritual distress were a chemical event. I'm not opposed to the judicious use of medications, but isn't it odd that, with all these wonderful anti-depressants available, suicide rates in the U.S. have risen 33 percent in the last twenty years?

When you adopt this materialist worldview, madness follows with perfect logic. If you're a man but want to be a woman, you need only mutilate your flesh and take hormones, and it will be so. If you're a meat puppet plus a chemistry set, change the meat, change the chemistry, and you have changed everything. It makes sense that a baby can be slaughtered without conscience. What is it, after all, what are any of us but a cluster of dividing cells? Meat. Chemistry. Communism makes sense — because a nation of slaves who all have the same amount of money is more practical than a nation of free men who experience some natural inequality. What good is freedom to a meat puppet? What does a meat puppet need besides meat?

All the nonsense our elites believe is logical in a godless world. It only seems insane because it is insane. Because we don't live in a godless world. Their logic is not built on the facts. Their reality is not real.

How then do we begin to speak into the madhouse that is our current culture?

Again, I think my own life provides the example. If God Himself could lay aside His holy name to speak into my despair, then we too can have the humility to make our arguments from the ground up.

This does not mean we should fall for the lie that a secular outlook is somehow the neutral default setting of public discourse. Secularism is a cult. It endangers our freedoms because it attempts to solve spiritual problems by increasingly oppressive, materialistic, and political means. Socialism replaces charity. Enforced inclusion replaces love of neighbor. MeToo anger and legalism replace manly honor and womanly virtue. Climate panic replaces eschatology. And on and on. We can't pretend to join that cult of secularism. But we can learn to present God in ways that secular people can understand if they choose.

This is not a solution religious people like to hear. A few years ago, a well-heeled Christian organization invited me to appear on a discussion panel with other Christian artists. We were asked the question: What is the mission of a Christian artist in our time? I replied that I would be happy if I could convince thinking people that there is such a thing as truth. The writer next to me became livid. He scolded me. He told me there was only one truth, Jesus Christ, and that it was our job to preach that truth to those who did not believe. He spoke so angrily that he later came up to me and apologized — but I was the one who was never invited back to speak to that group again.

That actually made sense to me. What he was saying was appealing and comforting. What I was saying was tragic and hard. I was telling them just how bad things are. I was saying to them that we have lost the fight at the highest levels of our intellectual culture. God is dead there. Not dead, in fact, of course, but dead to our best minds as he was once dead to me. Within my lifetime, a charismatic evangelist like Billy Graham could preach Jesus to the man on the street and start a revival. A heroic pope like John Paul II could declare Christ to the nations and the walls of their unbelief would come tumbling down. They had the power of a tradition behind them, a Bible full of stories everyone knew, a history of deep intellectual arguments that the very name of Jesus Christ expressed. Those Bible stories have been erased from our curricula and forgotten. Those arguments have been demonized and silenced. We have to tell those stories again. We have to make those arguments again.

I am speaking from my experience. I didn't come to God because I discovered God. I couldn't discover Him. He was forbidden to exist under the intellectual rules of my culture. I came to God because I discovered that those rules were falsehoods. I came to God because, through stories and reasoning, I discovered there was such a thing as truth and from that discovery, faith logically, inexorably followed.

When I speak at universities, I sometimes tell the students that all Western Civilization was built on the shoulders of two men: Socrates and Jesus. These two men had a good deal in common. Both were born into a time when many sophisticated people believed that there was no such thing as moral truth. Both men believed in moral truth, but both also knew that the truth is subtle and has to be approached by half measures. Socrates approached truth by asking people questions until the received wisdom of their culture collapsed into the nonsense it was. Jesus approached the truth by telling parables, and by becoming a living parable himself.

If we have lost the basis of our civilization — if the Imago Dei, the source of human dignity, is now thought incompatible with human dignity — then we must go back to the beginning. We must imitate Socrates and Jesus. We must ask questions and tell stories ourselves.

In the universities, on the news sites, in podcasts, and debates, we should put aside the language of self-certainty, outrage, and condemnation, and take up the Socratic language of inquiry. If you believe there is no absolute good or evil, and that therefore all cultures are morally equal, how then can it be evil to hate another culture, there being no evil or good in the first place? If gender is a construct and there is no essential difference between men and women, then when a man is a woman on the inside, how does he know?

Likewise, we must learn to tell stories, write novels, make movies and TV shows, that speak to people where they are. This is why I disagree with religious people when they say, for instance, that there is too much sex and profanity and violence in today's art and entertainment. As an artist, my job is to represent the world as it is, and there are times I can't do that without sex and profanity and violence. What matters is that in those stories that step into the dark side of existence, the darkness operates like an arrow pointing to the light.

In my case, for instance, it was reading Dostoevsky's novel *Crime and Punishment* that began my long turn away from moral relativism. It's a grim tale of an axe murderer who falls in love with a prostitute. Go into a Christian bookstore today and ask the clerk for a book about an axe murderer who falls for a hooker and see what it gets you. They specialize in affirmation and consolation because they are speaking to fellow Christians. Fair enough. But you can't say Jesus, Jesus, Jesus, to those who are repelled by the sound of His name. We must do as He did and go to them where they are.

Socrates and Jesus should be our guides to rebuilding the culture they built in the first place. And when we are attacked for this, damned, banned, fired, and all the rest, we should remember one more similarity between these two men.

Both were assassinated by the powers that be — both had to die before their philosophies reshaped the intellectual landscape. If we have lost the world their wisdom made, if we must begin again at the beginning, then, like Socrates and Jesus, we must enter the marketplace, the classroom, the theater, and the tavern where the young sinners gather. Like Socrates and Jesus, we are going to have to ask questions and tell stories.

And as for the consequences, like Socrates and Jesus, we're going to have to take our chances.

ANDREW KLAVAN is the author of such internationally bestselling crime novels as *True Crime*, filmed by Clint Eastwood, *Don't Say A Word*, filmed starring Michael Douglas, as well as *Empire of Lies* and *Werewolf Cop*. He has been nominated for the Mystery Writers of America's Edgar Award five times and has won twice. He wrote the screenplays to "A Shock to The System," which starred Michael Caine, "One Missed Call," which starred Edward Burns, and "Gosnell: The Trial of America's Biggest Serial Killer," starring Dean Cain. His political satire videos have been viewed by tens of millions of people, and he currently hosts a popular podcast, "The Andrew Klavan Show," at the *Daily Wire*. His most recent non-fiction book, *The Great Good Thing: A Secular Jew Comes to Faith in Christ*, is a memoir of his religious journey. His most recent fiction is the fantasy suspense trilogy *Another Kingdom*.

Made in the USA
Coppell, TX
21 November 2019

11682337R00035